Topic 1 Scarcity and choice

The concept of the margin

Economists concentrate on decisions that are taken at the margin. For example, consumption decisions can be analysed in terms of marginal utility, which is the additional satisfaction that is gained from the consumption of one more unit of a product. It is important to distinguish between marginal utility, which is the additional satisfaction of consuming one more unit, and total utility, which is the total satisfaction of consuming a number of units.

Production decisions can be analysed in terms of marginal cost. This is the additional cost of producing one more unit of a product. It is important to distinguish

between marginal cost, which is the additional cost of producing one more unit, and total cost, which is the total cost of producing a number of units.

Rationality is where decisions are taken and choices are made on the basis of preferences. For example, consumer rationality is where a consumer chooses the feasible alternative that he or she most prefers. Where an alternative is chosen that is not the most preferred choice, this can be regarded as irrational. Rationality for a consumer is where products are chosen which provide the best value for money or the greatest benefit relative to cost.

1 **Explain what is meant by the concept of the margin. (AO2)**   4 marks

....

....

....

....

....

....

....

....

2 **Evaluate the extent to which the marginal concept is useful to economic agents in decision making. (AO4)**   12 marks

....

....

....

....

....

....

....

....

....

....

....

(Answer lines continue on page 4)

3 Evaluate the concept of rationality as a way of understanding the behaviour of households, firms and governments. (AO4)

OCR

A LEVEL YEAR 2

WORKBOOK

Economics

Microeconomics 2

Terry Cook

HODDER
EDUCATION
LEARN MORE

Contents

WORKBOOK

① This workbook will prepare you for OCR A-level H460/01 Microeconomics.

② The workbook focuses on these areas of study:
- scarcity and choice
- how competitive markets work
- competition and market power
- labour market
- market failure and government intervention

③ The examination is 2 hours long and you will need to answer a range of questions, some requiring relatively short answers and others requiring longer answers which need to be planned in the same way as essays. Some of these questions will only carry 2 or 4 marks, but some will carry as many as 25 marks.

④ For each topic you will find:
- stimulus material
- short-answer questions that build up to exam-style questions
- spaces for you to write or plan your answers
- questions that test your mathematical skills

⑤ Answering the questions will help you to build your skills and meet the assessment objectives AO1 (knowledge and understanding), AO2 (application), AO3 (analysis) and AO4 (evaluation).

⑥ You still need to read your textbook and refer to your revision guides and lesson notes.

⑦ Marks available are indicated for all questions so that you can gauge the level of detail required in your answers.

⑧ Timings are given for the exam-style questions to make your practice as realistic as possible.

⑨ Answers are available at:
www.hoddereducation.co.uk/workbookanswers.

Exam-style questions

4 **a** Calculate, from the table below, the marginal cost of producing 3,000 units of a product. (AO1)

2 marks ⑨

Output (units)	Total cost (£)	Marginal cost (£)
1,000	800	800
2,000	1,000	200
3,000	1,600	
4,000	2,800	1,200
5,000	4,400	1,600

b Explain why a firm would want to know the marginal cost of producing one more item of a product. (AO2)

4 marks

For multiple-choice questions, circle the letter of the answer that you think is correct.

5 The concept of the margin is based on which of the following? (AO1) **1 mark**

A Average profit derived by a producer

B Average utility derived by a consumer

C First unit produced or consumed

D Last unit produced or consumed

6 Rationality is based on the idea that a choice is made that results in which of the following? (AO1) **1 mark**

A The elimination of the economic problem

B The lowest possible price being paid for a product

C The optimal level of benefit for an individual

D The satisfaction of all needs and wants

Topic 2 How competitive markets work

Productive and allocative efficiency

The difference between productive and allocative efficiency was covered in Microeconomics 1. It is now necessary to introduce the concepts of static efficiency, dynamic efficiency and X-inefficiency.

Static efficiency is concerned with the most efficient combination of scarce resources in an economy, but at a given point in time. Both productive efficiency and allocative efficiency can be seen as elements of static efficiency.

Dynamic efficiency, however, goes beyond a particular point in time and takes into account how efficiency could be improved over time. This approach to the concept of efficiency stresses that, over time, better technology and more efficient working practices can contribute to greater efficiency of production.

The concept of X-inefficiency refers to what has been termed 'organisational slack' in a firm. This is where a firm may produce at higher than minimum cost, especially if such a firm is operating in a non-competitive market. In such a situation, a firm is not producing at the minimum point on its average cost curve. Unit costs are not being minimised because there is a lack of competition in the market, giving rise to a degree of inefficiency.

1 Distinguish between static and dynamic efficiency. (AO2) `4 marks`

....

....

....

....

....

....

....

2 Explain what is meant by X-inefficiency. (AO2) `4 marks`

....

....

....

....

....

....

....

3 Evaluate the importance of static efficiency and dynamic efficiency. (AO4)   12 marks

Exam-style questions

Carson & West plc

A furniture manufacturer, Carson & West plc, has just appointed a new chief executive officer. He has realised that the firm is not as efficient as it could, and should, be. Instead of focusing on short-term ways of improving efficiency in the firm, he has decided that the best way to move forward is to improve its efficiency in the long term, i.e. he sees improvements in dynamic efficiency, rather than improvements in static efficiency, as the answer.

4 Suggest ways in which the firm could plan to improve its level of efficiency over a period of time. (AO2) **4 marks** ⑥

....

....

....

....

....

....

....

....

....

....

....

....

....

....

For multiple-choice questions, circle the letter of the answer that you think is correct.

5 Productive and allocative efficiency are examples of which of the following? (AO1) **1 mark**

A Dynamic efficiency

B Static efficiency

C Super-normal efficiency

D X-efficiency

6 When does dynamic efficiency take place? (AO1) **1 mark**

A At a given moment in time

B In the past

C In the private sector only

D Over a period of time

Topic 3 Competition and market power

Business objectives

Profit maximisation

Firms may have a variety of business objectives. Traditionally, the most important of these has been profit maximisation. This is when a firm's output is at the point where marginal cost is equal to marginal revenue. The theory of the firm is based on this underlying assumption, but it does raise two important points. First, will a firm have the necessary information to identify this profit-maximising position correctly? Second, is it not possible that some firms may have other business objectives?

1 **Explain profit maximisation as a business objective. (AO2)** `4 marks`

....

....

....

....

2 **Evaluate the relevance of profit maximisation to a business. (AO4)** `12 marks`

....

....

....

....

....

....

....

....

....

....

....

....

....

....

....

....

Alternative maximisation objectives for a business

There are other possible maximisation objectives that a firm may have. These can include the following:

- sales revenue maximisation
- sales volume maximisation
- growth maximisation
- utility maximisation

---

3 Evaluate possible alternative maximisation objectives for businesses, other than profit maximisation. (AO4)　　**12 marks**

Non-maximising objectives for a firm

There are also non-maximising objectives that a firm may have. These can include the following:

- profit satisficing
- social welfare
- ethical goals
- corporate social responsibility

4 Evaluate possible non-maximising objectives for businesses. (AO4)   `12 marks`

....

....

....

....

....

....

....

....

....

....

....

....

....

....

Choice of objectives and the principal–agent problem

There are a number of factors that can influence the choice of objectives by a firm, such as who owns the firm, who manages the firm, how large the firm is, what the firm's competitors are doing and the time period under consideration.

The principal–agent problem shows that there can be a possible conflict between the owners and the managers of a firm. The owners, i.e. the principal, may establish certain objectives, but it may be difficult for them to check that the appointed managers, i.e. the agent, adopt policies that are consistent with these objectives.

5 Explain what is meant by the principal–agent problem. (AO2)   `4 marks`

....

....

....

....

Market structures and their implications for the way resources are allocated and the interdependence of firms

Diminishing returns

The law of diminishing returns, or law of variable proportions as it is also known, states that when additional units of a variable factor of production are added to a fixed factor of production, total output increases but less than proportionately.

---

6 **Explain the law of diminishing returns. (AO2)**   4 marks

....

....

....

....

....

....

....

Perfect competition

Perfect competition has a number of characteristics:

- there are many buyers and sellers, all of whom are price takers

- all products are homogeneous, so that firms cannot attempt to differentiate their product

- buyers and sellers have perfect knowledge and perfect information, so that they know the products that are being sold in the market and at what price

- factors of production are perfectly mobile

- the individual firm can make supernormal profits or losses in the short run

- there are no barriers of entry into, or exit from, the industry

- the individual firm can only earn normal profits in the long run

- the individual firm will be allocatively efficient

- the individual firm will be productively efficient in the long run

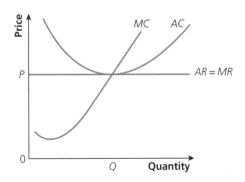

Figure 1 Perfect competition in the long run

7 Explain the characteristics of perfect competition. (AO2)   4 marks

....
....
....
....
....
....
....
....
....
....
....

8 Explain, with the aid of a diagram, why the individual firm in perfect competition is a price taker. (AO2)   4 marks

....
....
....
....
....
....
....
....
....
....
....
....
....
....
....

9 Explain, with the aid of a diagram, why the individual firm in perfect competition can make supernormal profits or losses in the short run, but only earn normal profits in the long run. (AO2)

....
....
....
....
....
....
....
....
....
....
....
....
....
....
....
....

Monopoly

Monopoly has a number of characteristics:

- it is a situation where there is a single seller in a market

- a business with monopoly power is a price maker, rather than a price taker

- a monopolist can make supernormal profits in both the short run and the long run; this is because of the existence of barriers to entry which prevent supernormal profits being competed away

- a profit-maximising monopolist may be neither allocatively nor productively efficient

- a business with monopoly power can practise price discrimination

- a monopoly faces a downward-sloping demand curve, so a monopolist can set the price or the output, but not both

- a monopolist will need to lower the price to sell an additional unit of a product

- marginal revenue is below average revenue because of the price being reduced on all previous units

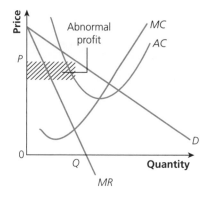

Figure 2 Monopoly

10 Explain the characteristics of monopoly. (AO2)

4 marks

....
....
....
....
....
....
....
....
....

It is important to distinguish between a monopoly and a natural monopoly and a monopoly and a monopsony. Whereas a monopoly is a single-firm industry, a natural monopoly develops when one firm has sufficient technical economies of scale to satisfy market demand more efficiently than two or more firms. In such a situation, the demand curve intersects the firm's average cost curve when it is still falling or at its lowest point.

Whereas a monopoly refers to a single seller, a monopsony refers to a single buyer of a product or of a factor of production. The term is most commonly used in labour markets.

11 Explain, with the aid of a diagram, what is meant by a natural monopoly. (AO2)

4 marks

....
....
....
....
....
....
....
....
....
....
....

12 Describe a monopsony. (AO1)

2 marks

Price discrimination

It is possible for a monopolist to charge different prices for the same product, as long as the following conditions apply:

- the monopolist is able to separate a market into different segments
- these segments have different price elasticities of demand
- the monopoly firm is able to prevent resale between the different segments of the market

13 Explain, with the aid of a diagram, what is meant by price discrimination by a business with monopoly power. (AO2)

4 marks

Barriers to entry and exit

One of the features of different market structures that can influence how firms behave is the existence or absence of barriers to entry into, and barriers to exit from, markets. Such barriers can include the following:

- legislation, such as when the state gives a firm monopoly status in a market

- product differentiation through marketing and branding

- control over retail outlets

- patents and trademarks

- control over supplies

- a cost advantage, such as through economies of scale

14 **Explain what is meant by barriers to entry and exit. (AO2)** `4 marks`

....
....
....
....
....
....
....
....

Monopolistic competition

Monopolistic competition has a number of characteristics:

- there are a number of sellers in the market

- the products sold are differentiated, e.g. there is an emphasis on branding

- there are no, or very weak, barriers to entry into, or exit from, the industry

- firms can make abnormal profits in the short run, but these are competed away in the long run as firms enter the industry

- in the long run, firms can only make normal profits

- in the long run, the firm is productively inefficient

- in the long run, the firm is allocatively inefficient

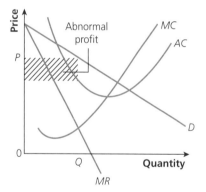

Figure 3(a) Monopolistic competition in the short run

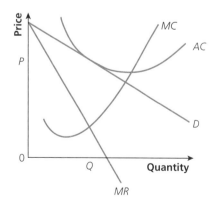

Figure 3(b) Monopolistic competition in the long run

15 Explain the characteristics of monopolistic competition. (AO2)

4 marks

Oligopoly

Oligopoly has a number of characteristics:

- a few firms dominate the market (if two firms dominate a market, it is known as a duopoly)

- the concentration ratio is very high

- the actions of one firm can have a significant effect on the behaviour of other firms in the market

- a firm's behaviour will be influenced by what it thinks other firms are going to do

- there is no one price or output in oligopoly

- firms are interdependent

- with just a few firms in a market, they often collude

- prices often stay the same and so there is a great deal of non-price competition

- product differentiation is significant in oligopoly

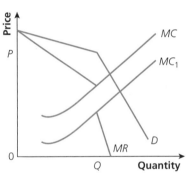

Figure 4 Oligopoly: the kinked demand curve

16 Explain the characteristics of oligopoly. (AO2)

4 marks

17 Explain what is meant by non-price competition. (AO2)   4 marks

....

....

....

....

....

....

....

....

....

....

....

Contestable markets

A perfectly contestable market has a number of characteristics:

- there is freedom of entry and exit, i.e. there are no barriers to entry or exit

- the costs of entry and exit are zero

- it is the threat of other firms entering the market that is significant; firms already in the market face a constant threat of increasing competition

- there is a lot of pressure on firms to act competitively, so there are likely to be low prices, good-quality service, a high level of choice and high output

- sunk costs, i.e. costs already invested in the industry which cannot be recovered, can be ignored

- hit-and-run competition can occur rather than competition throughout the market

- the number of firms competing in such a market will vary

- firms will compete rather than collude

- abnormal profits are earned in the short run

- normal profits are earned in the long run

18 Explain the characteristics of a perfectly contestable market. (AO2)   4 marks

....

....

....

....

....

....

....

....

....

....

....

19 Explain why a business in a perfectly contestable market will be both allocatively and productively efficient. (AO2)

4 marks

....

....

....

....

....

....

....

Integration

Integration can take three different forms.

Horizontal integration is where a merger or takeover involves two or more firms that are at the same stage of production.

Vertical integration is where a merger or takeover involves two or more firms that are at different stages of production. There are two types of such integration.

Backward vertical integration is where the merger or takeover involves a supplier, i.e. it is an earlier stage. Forward vertical integration is where the merger or takeover involves a distributor, i.e. it is a later stage.

Conglomerate integration is where a merger or takeover involves two or more firms that are unrelated. The firms will be diverse as a result of a deliberate attempt to reduce the risk associated with specialisation in one particular industry.

20 Distinguish between horizontal and vertical integration. (AO1)

2 marks

....

....

....

21 Explain what is meant by conglomerate integration. (AO2)

4 marks

....

....

....

....

....

....

....

The growth of firms

The growth of firms can come about in two main ways. External growth comes about through integration with other firms. This can be through a merger, a takeover or an acquisition. Internal growth comes about through the expansion of a firm so that it is able to produce and sell more goods and/or services.

There are a number of aims that can influence the growth of firms. These include the following:

- the ability to benefit from economies of scale

- the desire to gain a greater share of a market and therefore obtain more market power

- to make it less likely that a firm will be a merger target of another firm

- in the case of a conglomerate, the aim could be to reduce risk through diversification by operating in a different market

22 **Analyse the factors which influence the growth of firms. (AO3)**   12 marks

Exam-style questions

23 Evaluate the possible factors which could influence the choice of objectives by businesses. (AO4) **25 marks** **38**

24 Explain, with the aid of a diagram, the equilibrium price and the equilibrium output for a firm in perfect competition in the long run. (AO2) **4 marks** 6

25 Explain, with the aid of a diagram, the equilibrium price and the equilibrium output for a profit-maximising monopolist. (AO2) **4 marks** 6

26 Evaluate, with the aid of a diagram, the usefulness of perfect competition theory. (AO4)

25 marks 38

27 Evaluate, with the aid of a diagram, the advantages and disadvantages of monopoly power. (AO4)

25 marks   38

28 Explain, with the aid of a diagram, why a business in monopolistic competition can make supernormal profits or losses in the short run, but only normal profits in the long run. (AO2) **4 marks** 6

....

....

....

....

....

....

....

....

....

....

....

....

....

....

....

....

....

....

....

29 The table below shows the six firms in a market and their share of the market.

Firm	Share of market (%)
Firm A	42
Firm B	26
Firm C	14
Firm D	10
Firm E	5
Firm F	3

a Calculate the four-firm concentration ratio in this market. (AO1) **2 marks** 9

....

b Explain the meaning of a concentration ratio. (AO2) **4 marks**

....

....

....

30 Explain the significance of interdependence in oligopoly markets. (AO2)   **4 marks**   6

....

....

....

....

....

....

....

31 Evaluate, with the aid of a diagram, the advantages and disadvantages of a perfectly contestable market. (AO4)   **12 marks**   18

....

....

....

....

....

....

....

....

....

....

....

....

....

....

....

....

....

....

....

For multiple-choice questions, circle the letter of the answer that you think is correct.

32 Profit maximisation occurs where: (AO1)   `1 mark`

   A $MC = AC$

   B $MC = AR$

   C $MC = MR$

   D $MC = TC$

33 In perfect competition, firms earn which of the following in the long
run? (AO1)   `1 mark`

   A Abnormal loss

   B Abnormal profit

   C Normal profit

   D Supernormal profit

34 In monopoly, what is the relationship between marginal revenue and average
revenue? (AO1)   `1 mark`

   A Marginal revenue is above average revenue

   B Marginal revenue is below average revenue

   C Marginal revenue is discontinuous whereas average revenue is kinked

   D Marginal revenue is equal to average revenue

35 NatWest was formed in 1968 as a result of the merger of the National Provincial
Bank and Westminster Bank. This is an example of which of the following
types of integration? (AO1)   `1 mark`

   A Backward vertical integration

   B Conglomerate integration

   C Forward vertical integration

   D Horizontal integration

36 Which of the following defines a perfectly contestable market? A market in
which: (AO1)   `1 mark`

   A firms earn supernormal profits in the long run

   B firms will collude rather than compete

   C sunk costs need to be taken into account

   D there are no barriers to entry or exit

Topic 4 Labour market

Wage determination

The demand for labour

The demand for labour is usually described as a derived demand. This means that employers do not require labour for its own sake, but for what it can contribute to the production of a final product.

Although the demand for labour is often referred to, there are actually many sub-markets in an economy, each with particular features that affect the demand for labour in that sub-market.

One of the main factors that can affect the demand for labour is the wage elasticity of demand for labour, i.e. how responsive the demand for labour is in relation to a change in the wages paid to labour.

It is important to distinguish between a nominal or money wage, which does not take into account the rate of inflation in an economy, and a real wage, which has been adjusted to take into account the impact of inflation on a particular wage.

1 **Explain the concept of the derived demand for labour. (AO2)**   4 marks

....

....

....

....

....

....

....

....

2 **Explain the difference between nominal and real wages. (AO2)**   4 marks

....

....

....

....

....

....

....

....

Productivity

Productivity refers to the output produced per factor of production over a given period of time, i.e. it measures the efficiency with which resources are used. Labour productivity therefore refers to the output per worker per period of time.

Labour productivity can be increased through the following ways:

- more training and education
- better capital equipment arising from increased capital investment
- better management and improved management techniques
- improved technology as a result of technological change

---

3 **Explain what is meant by productivity. (AO2)** 4 marks

....

....

....

....

....

....

....

....

Unit labour costs

Unit labour costs are related to the concept of productivity. They measure the average cost of labour per unit of output and are calculated as the ratio of total labour costs to real output.

---

4 **Describe unit labour costs. (AO1)** 2 marks

....

....

....

....

....

Human capital

Labour is sometimes described as human capital, especially when it is not just the quantity of labour that is being considered but also the quality. Human capital refers to the knowledge and skills acquired by workers. It is an important concept because the better the quality of human capital, the more productive a worker is likely to be.

5 Explain what is meant by human capital. (AO2)   4 marks

....

....

....

....

....

....

....

The supply of labour

The supply of labour to a particular industry can be affected by a number of factors, which can be both monetary and non-monetary. One important factor is the wage elasticity of supply of labour. It is also important to understand the difference between the short-run and the long-run supply of labour.

6 Explain the factors that can affect the supply of labour in a particular industry. (AO2)   4 marks

....

....

....

....

....

....

....

Economic rent and transfer earnings

Transfer earnings refer to the amount of money that a factor of production needs to earn to keep it employed in its present use in the long run. It means the money that could be earned in the best alternative employment.

Economic rent refers to the amount of money that is paid to a factor of production over and above its transfer earnings, i.e. what it could earn elsewhere.

The total payment to a factor of production, such as labour, can therefore be divided between these two parts. In Figure 5, *BWA* shows the economic rent and *0QAB* shows the transfer earnings.

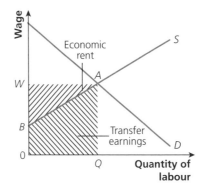

Figure 5 Economic rent and transfer earnings

31

7 Explain, with the aid of a diagram, the difference between economic rent and transfer earnings. (AO2)

....
....
....
....
....
....

Wage determination in a highly competitive labour market

In a highly competitive labour market, there are many firms and many workers. Each firm is a wage taker, i.e. it can employ as many workers as it wishes at a given wage rate. In such a labour market, wages will be determined by the market forces of the demand for, and the supply of, labour.

Figure 6(a) shows how the wage in the industry is determined and Figure 6(b) shows that each individual firm in the industry is a wage taker, the number of workers employed by the firm being determined by the demand curve which represents the marginal revenue product of the workers.

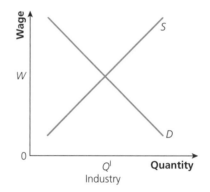

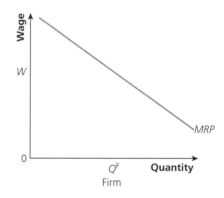

Figures 6(a) and (b) Wage determination in a highly competitive labour market

8 Explain, with the aid of a diagram, how wages are determined in a highly competitive labour market. (AO2)

....
....
....
....
....
....

The impact of trade union activity on labour markets

A trade union can have an impact on labour markets. A trade union can use its power to increase the price, i.e. the wage, of labour. Figure 7 shows that without trade union intervention, the equilibrium wage would be $0W$. However, the trade union can bargain on behalf of its members and negotiate a higher wage rate of $0W_1$.

The problem, however, is that whereas $0Q$ workers would have been employed at a wage of $0W$, only $0Q_1$ workers will be employed at the higher wage of $0W_1$.

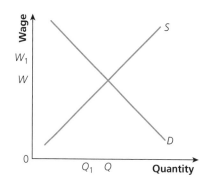

Figure 7 The impact of trade union activity on labour markets

9 **Evaluate, with the aid of a diagram, the impact of trade union activity on labour markets. (AO4)**

12 marks

The impact of a monopsonist employer on a labour market

The distinction between a monopolist and a monopsonist has already been referred to earlier in this Workbook. Whereas a monopoly refers to a single seller, a monopsony refers to a single buyer of a product or of a factor of production.

In a labour market, monopsonist employers can be recognised in three ways:

- they are major employers of labour and so have power over the labour market

- they are wage makers, not wage takers

- they face an upward-sloping supply curve because they need to increase the wage rate to attract more

workers; they need to increase the wage for the last worker employed and for all previous workers, so that the marginal cost of labour is higher than the average cost of labour.

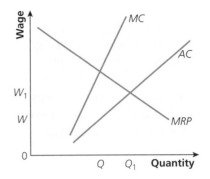

Figure 8 The impact of a monopsonist employer on a labour market

---

⑩ **Evaluate, with the aid of a diagram, the impact of a monopsonist employer on a labour market. (AO4)**　　　　　12 marks

The impact of a bilateral monopoly on a labour market

This situation occurs when a single or monopoly buyer of labour, i.e. a monopsonist, faces a single or monopoly seller of labour, i.e. a trade union. Each will have a great deal of influence on a labour market and the actual outcome will depend on the relative bargaining strength of each side.

Labour market issues and themes

There are some key concepts in relation to the labour market:

- The **labour force** refers to the number of people who are available for work in an economy at a given moment in time.

- The **working population** refers to those people who are working or who are actively seeking employment, i.e. it includes both the employed and the unemployed.

- The **participation rate** refers to the proportion of a country's population which is either in employment or officially registered as unemployed.

- The **dependency ratio** is the ratio of those people in a country who are unable to work divided by the total working age population.

- The **replacement ratio** is the percentage of working income that an individual needs to maintain the same standard of living in retirement.

⑪ **Describe the working population. (AO1)** `2 marks`

....
....
....
....
....
....

It is possible to distinguish between the national minimum wage and the living wage.

⑫ **Distinguish between the national minimum wage and the living wage. (AO1)** `2 marks`

....
....
....
....
....

Trade union activity has already been referred to in relation to wage determination. Workers can be represented by trade unions in wage negotiations through collective bargaining and productivity bargaining.

---

13 **Distinguish between collective bargaining and productivity bargaining. (AO1)** `2 marks`

....

....

....

....

Labour markets can also be affected by other factors. Migration can lead to an increase in population and therefore an increase in the working population when net migration is positive, i.e. more people are coming to a country than are leaving it. Other demographic changes can also have an impact on labour markets, such as changes in the size of families or changes in the age distribution of a country's population. The existence of discrimination can also have an impact on labour markets, although legislation can be passed in an attempt to reduce the significance of this, such as the Sex Discrimination Act of 1970 and the Equal Pay Act of 1975.

A flexible labour market is important in an economy as it will enable workers to move from one part of the country to another and/or from one occupation to another. Government policies have been introduced to increase labour flexibility by reducing the extent of geographical and occupational immobility of labour.

Government intervention

Income and wealth inequality

Income inequality refers to the extent to which income is distributed unevenly among a country's population. Individual, household and family income includes the revenue from wages, salaries, interest, dividends, rent, profits and transfer payments.

Wealth inequality is broader than income inequality and refers to the unequal distribution of financial assets among a country's population. Wealth includes the value of homes, motor vehicles, personal possessions, businesses, savings and investments.

---

14 **In terms of wealth, describe the meaning of investments. (AO1)** `2 marks`

....

....

....

....

15 **Distinguish between income equality and wealth inequality. (AO1)** `2 marks`

....

....

....

....

Government intervention in the labour market

A government can intervene in a labour market in a number of different ways, including:

- policies on pensions
- policies on migration
- policies on education and training
- policies on the tax and benefit system

16 Explain how a government could intervene in a labour market. (AO2) **4 marks**

....

....

....

....

....

....

....

....

....

....

....

Exam-style questions

17 Explain the factors that can affect the demand for labour in a particular industry. (AO2) **4 marks** **6**

....

....

....

....

....

....

....

....

....

....

....

18 Evaluate, with the aid of a diagram, the impact of a bilateral monopoly on a labour market. (AO4)

12 marks   18

19 Explain the reasons why wage differentials exist in an economy. (AO2)

4 marks   6

20 Explain, with the aid of a diagram, how a government can establish a minimum wage. (AO2)

4 marks · 6

....

....

....

....

....

....

....

....

....

....

21 a Calculate from the table below the proportion of wealth that is owned by the poorest 50% of the population. (AO1)

2 marks · 15

% of population	% of total UK wealth
Top 1%	21%
Top 2%	28%
Top 5%	40%
Top 10%	53%
Top 25%	72%
Top 50%	93%

....

b Analyse how a government could try to reduce income and wealth inequality in a country. (AO3)

8 marks

....

....

....

....

....

....

....

....

....

....

....

For multiple-choice questions, circle the letter of the answer that you think is correct.

22 A real wage takes into account which of the following? (AO1)   1 mark

   A   The exchange rate

   B   The productivity rate

   C   The rate of inflation

   D   The rate of unemployment

23 Which best defines the productivity of labour? (AO1)   1 mark

   A   Output per machine per hour

   B   Output per worker

   C   Output per worker per hour

   D   Total output of a firm's labour force

24 A monopsonist refers to which of the following? (AO1)   1 mark

   A   A highly productive worker

   B   A member of a large trade union

   C   A single buyer of labour

   D   A single seller of labour

25 Which of the following statements is correct? (AO1)   1 mark

   A   Both the minimum wage and the living wage are established through legislation.

   B   Neither the minimum wage nor the living wage is established through legislation.

   C   The living wage is established through legislation but not the minimum wage.

   D   The minimum wage is established through legislation but not the living wage.

26 What does *MRP* mean? (AO1)   1 mark

   A   Average cost of labour

   B   Demand curve for labour

   C   Supply curve of labour

   D   Total cost of labour

Topic 5 Market failure and government intervention

Public goods

The characteristics of public goods were covered in Microeconomics 1, but one additional characteristic needs to be mentioned here. No price is paid for a public good because supply is at zero marginal cost.

It is possible to distinguish between a private good — a good that is bought and consumed by individuals for their own benefit, and a public good — a good that is provided by the public sector, and which would not otherwise be provided.

The existence of public goods results in a free-rider problem. This is where an individual cannot be excluded from consuming a good or service, and therefore has no incentive to pay for the provision of such a good or service. Street lighting can be regarded as an example of a public good. No private firm would have an incentive to provide it if it was impossible to charge a price for it.

1 Explain what is meant when a public good is provided at zero marginal cost. (AO2)   4 marks

2 Explain what is meant by a quasi-public good. (AO2)   4 marks

Inequity

The inequality of income and wealth in societies has already been referred to. One of the main reasons for such inequality is differences in people's access to resources. These differences can be extremely significant in explaining the inequality of income and wealth in various countries.

The labour market provides one reason for inequalities in earned income, with unequal incomes arising from the demand and supply conditions in different labour markets. The differences between economic rent and transfer earnings in various economic sectors also explain such inequalities. Variations in the skills, education and training of different workers can explain why some earn much more than others.

Inequality of wealth and asset ownership can develop over a long period of time, especially through inheritance. The inequality has been made worse by the fact that homeowners gain, especially when house prices increase significantly, compared with those who rent their property, either from a private landlord or from a council.

---

3 **Explain the causes of inequality and wealth. (AO2)**   4 marks

....

....

....

....

....

....

....

Environment

The environment has three functions:

- provider of resources
- provider of amenities
- absorber of waste

Externalities can arise from both the impact of production and the impact of consumption on the environment, causing market failure.

The environmental Kuznets curve shows the relationship between environmental quality and economic development. Economic growth and increases in income per capita are associated with environmental degradation and the situation gets worse, with a worsening of the environment, until a certain point is reached. Beyond this point, income per capita continues to increase but the level of environmental degradation falls and the environment improves. The environmental Kuznets curve, which is derived from indicators of environmental quality, such as water quality and air pollution, is thus an inverted U-shape.

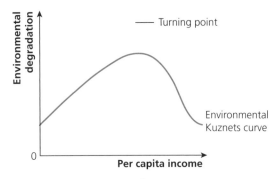

Figure 9 The environmental Kuznets curve

The environmental Kuznets curve has given rise to discussion as to whether economic growth will result in environmental degradation and resource depletion and so limit sustainable development. Sustainability can be defined as the capacity to endure, i.e. it is the endurance of particular systems and processes.

A range of different policies can be used to reduce the rate of environmental degradation and resource depletion. These can be at a local, national, regional and global level. Examples of such policies include:

- indirect taxation
- subsidies

- legislation and regulation, including environmental standards
- tradable pollution permits
- information provision
- government expenditure
- public and private partnerships

4 **Analyse how effective tradable pollution permits are likely to be in reducing the rate of environmental degradation and resource depletion. (AO3)**   8 marks

....
....
....
....
....
....
....
....
....
....

Alternative methods of government intervention

Microeconomics 1 dealt with a number of different ways in which a government could intervene in a market to correct or reduce market failure and inequity. These included taxation, subsidies, government expenditure, state provision, buffer stock systems, price controls, legislation and regulation, and information provision.

However, there are other possible methods that could be used and these include the following:

- public/private partnerships
- tradable pollution permits
- competition policy

Cost–benefit analysis

Cost–benefit analysis (CBA) is a way of measuring all the costs and benefits of a particular project or decision. The analysis will include private and external costs, and private and external benefits, so it can give a better indication of the true cost to society of a particular project.

The difficulty with CBA is that it is not always possible to give a monetary value to all the costs and benefits, and so shadow pricing is sometimes used to estimate the value of certain costs and/or benefits. Also, there are often third-party or spillover effects of a project, but it is not always easy to establish how far these extend.

CBA can be used in the assessment of infrastructure projects, such as in education, the environment, health and transport. The Victoria Line on the London Underground, the Channel Tunnel and various motorway projects are all examples of projects that have involved the carrying out of a CBA.

5 Explain what is meant by cost–benefit analysis. (AO2) 4 marks

....
....
....
....
....
....
....

Exam-style questions

6 Explain, with the aid of a diagram, the environmental Kuznets curve. (AO2) 4 marks 6

....
....
....
....
....
....
....
....
....
....
....

7 Explain how public/private partnerships could correct or reduce market failure and inequity in an economy. (AO2) 4 marks 6

....
....
....
....
....
....
....
....

8 Evaluate the value of cost–benefit analysis in helping governments to make decisions in situations where there is a market failure. (AO4)   **25 marks** 38

Third runway for Heathrow?

Plans have been put forward for the building of a third runway at Heathrow Airport. The cost of building the runway will be £18.6 billion. Supporters of the project claim that it will enable more planes, and therefore more passengers, to use the airport. New routes could be opened which would benefit people living in the UK and people coming to the country. It has been estimated that a third runway at Heathrow could boost the UK economy by £211 billion and create 70,000 new jobs.

Opponents of the project, however, have pointed out that it will create a great deal more noise, air pollution and traffic congestion in the area. In particular, opponents say that air quality in the area would be in breach of the EU's air quality directive. Over 4,000 homes will need to be demolished.

9 **Read the passage above and, using the information provided and any other information that you consider relevant, produce a cost–benefit analysis of the proposed construction of a third runway at Heathrow Airport. (AO3)** — 8 marks — 12

For multiple-choice questions, circle the letter of the answer that you think is correct.

⑩ A public good will be provided at: (AO1)

   A   negative marginal cost

   B   partial marginal cost

   C   positive marginal cost

   D   zero marginal cost

⑪ A bridge is best described as a: (AO1)

   A   demerit good

   B   merit good

   C   public good

   D   quasi-public good

⑫ Cost–benefit analysis takes into account: (AO1)

   A   private benefits only

   B   private costs and benefits only

   C   social benefits only

   D   social costs and benefits only

Also available

...and many more

Go to http://www.hoddereducation.co.uk/studentworkbooks for details of all our student workbooks.

Hodder Education, an Hachette UK company, Blenheim Court, George Street, Banbury, Oxfordshire OX16 5BH

Orders
Bookpoint Ltd, 130 Park Drive, Milton Park, Abingdon, Oxfordshire OX14 4SB
tel: 01235 827827
fax: 01235 400401
e-mail: education@bookpoint.co.uk
Lines are open 9.00 a.m.–5.00 p.m., Monday to Saturday, with a 24-hour message answering service.
You can also order through the Hodder Education website:
www.hoddereducation.co.uk
© Terry Cook 2016
ISBN 978-1-4718-4740-0
First printed 2016

Impression number	5	4	3	2	1
Year	2019	2018	2017	2016	

This guide has been written specifically to support students preparing for the OCR AS and A-level Economics examinations. The content has been neither approved nor endorsed by OCR and remains the sole responsibility of the author.

Typeset by Integra Software Services Pvt. Ltd., Pondicherry, India
Printed in Spain

Hachette UK's policy is to use papers that are natural, renewable and recyclable products and made from wood grown in sustainable forests. The logging and manufacturing processes are expected to conform to the environmental regulations of the country of origin.

HODDER
EDUCATION
AN HACHETTE UK COMPANY

ISBN 978-1-4718-4740-0

9 781471 847400